Different Types of Art
© Copyright 2019 by Harry Schad
All Rights Reserved
ISBN: 9781695882492
Harry-O-Graphs

Different Types of Art

written & illustrated by

Harry Schad

Chapter 1 = Basic Types of Art Form

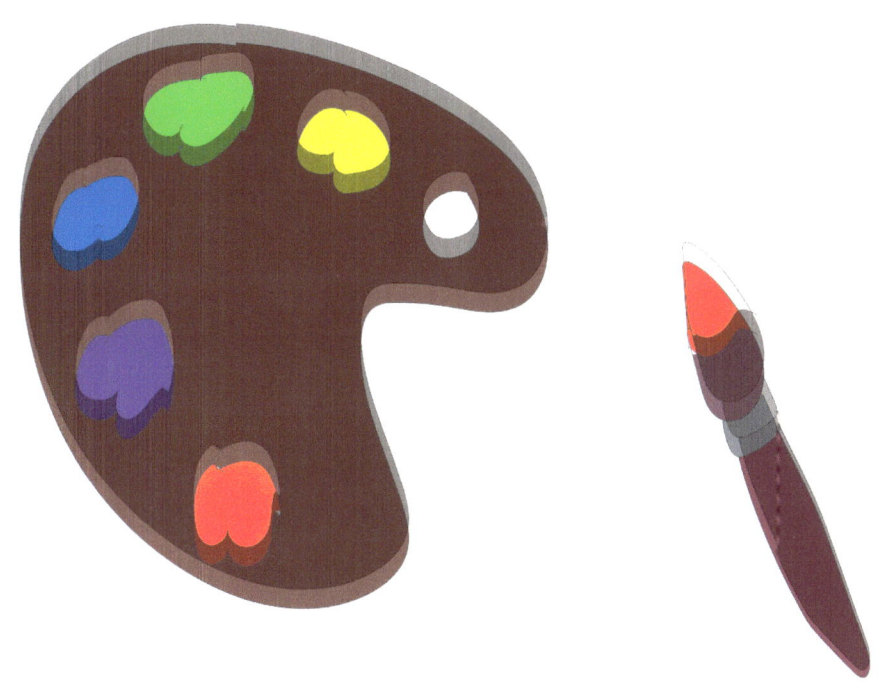

Drawing

Painting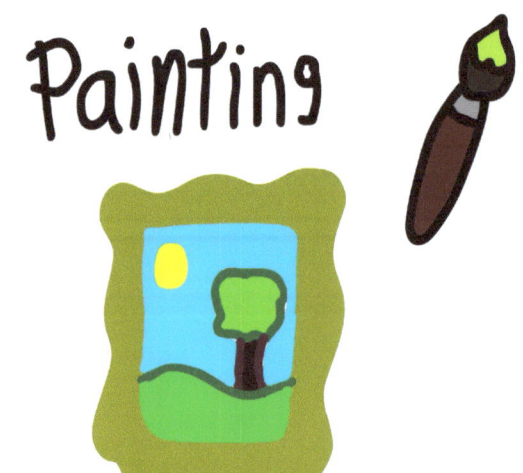

Sculpting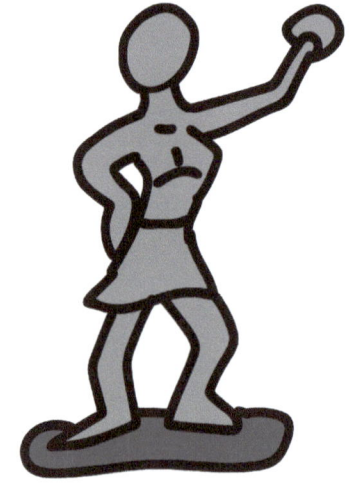

Modern art

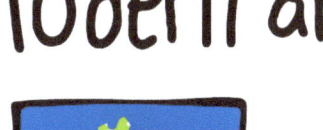

Abstract Art

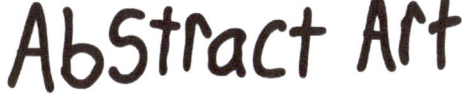

Impressionism

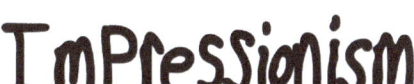

Cubism art

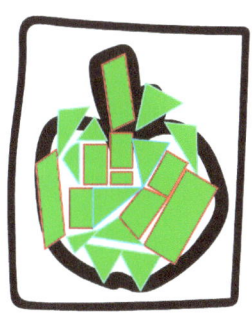

Surrealism art

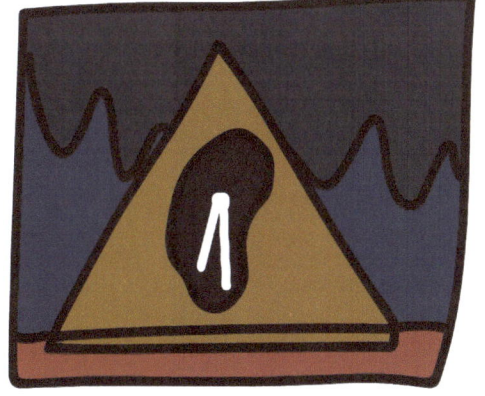

Chapter 2
Basic Colors

Primary Colors

Red

Blue

Yellow

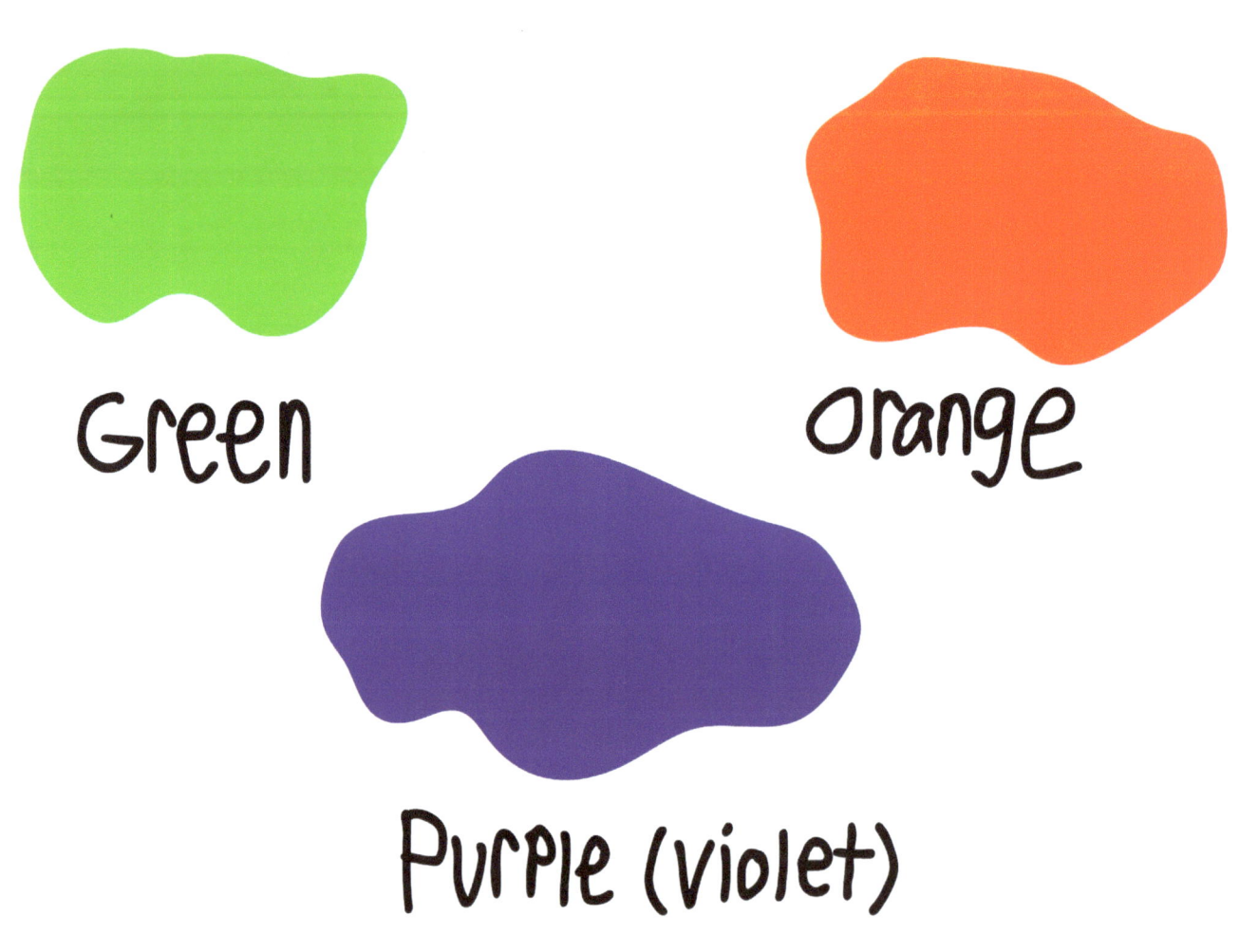

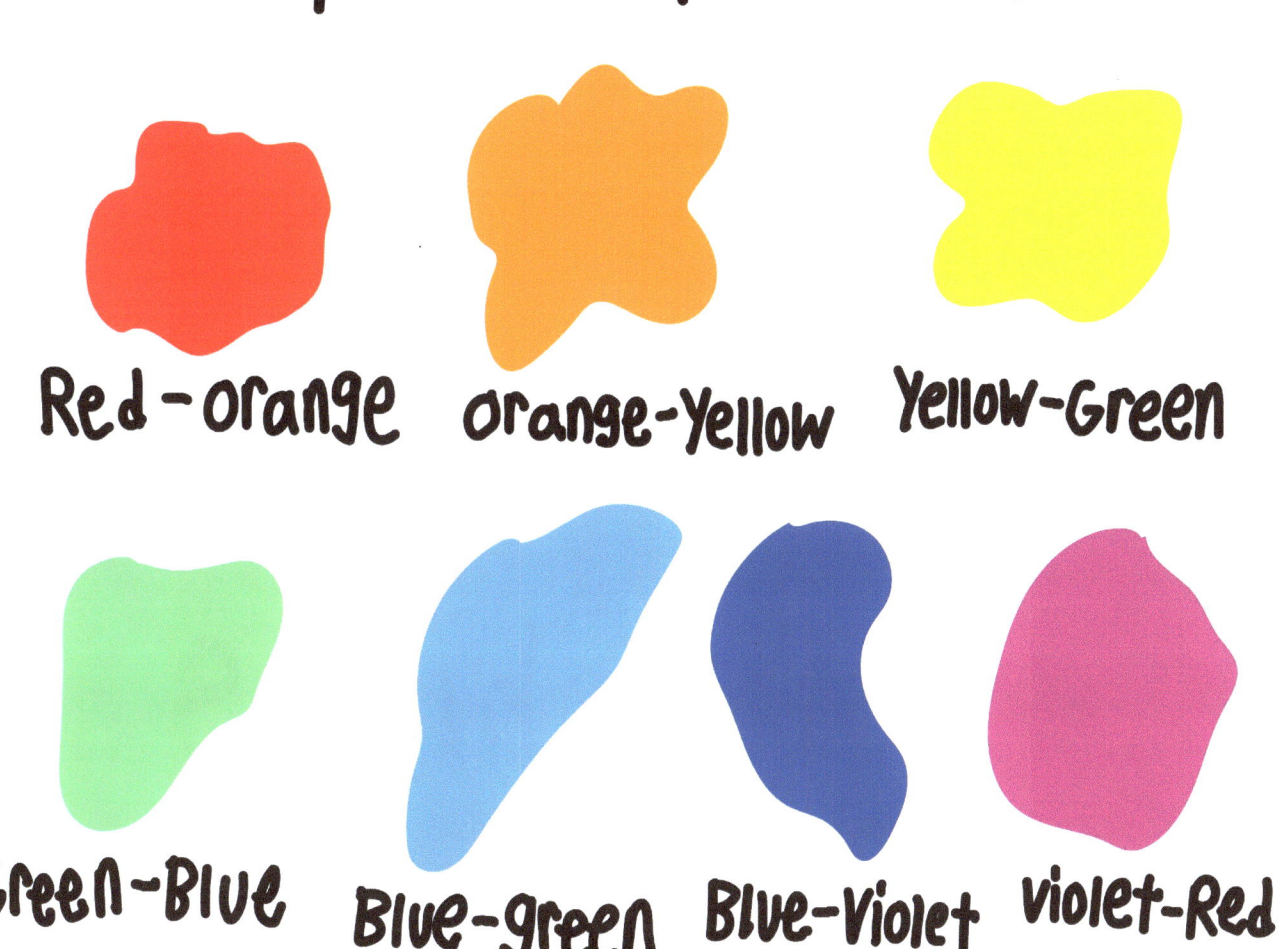

Chapter 3

Different Types of Shapes

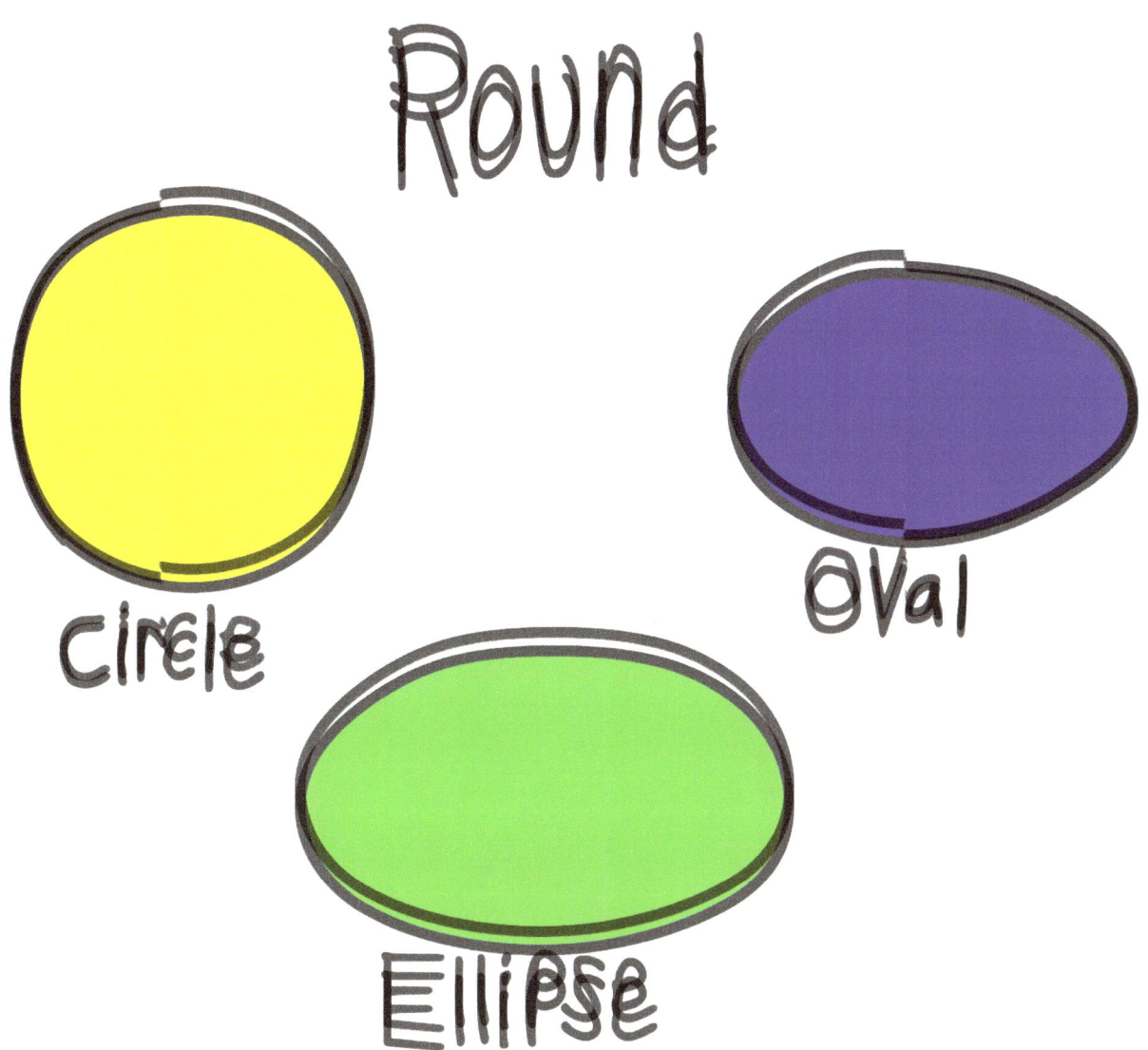

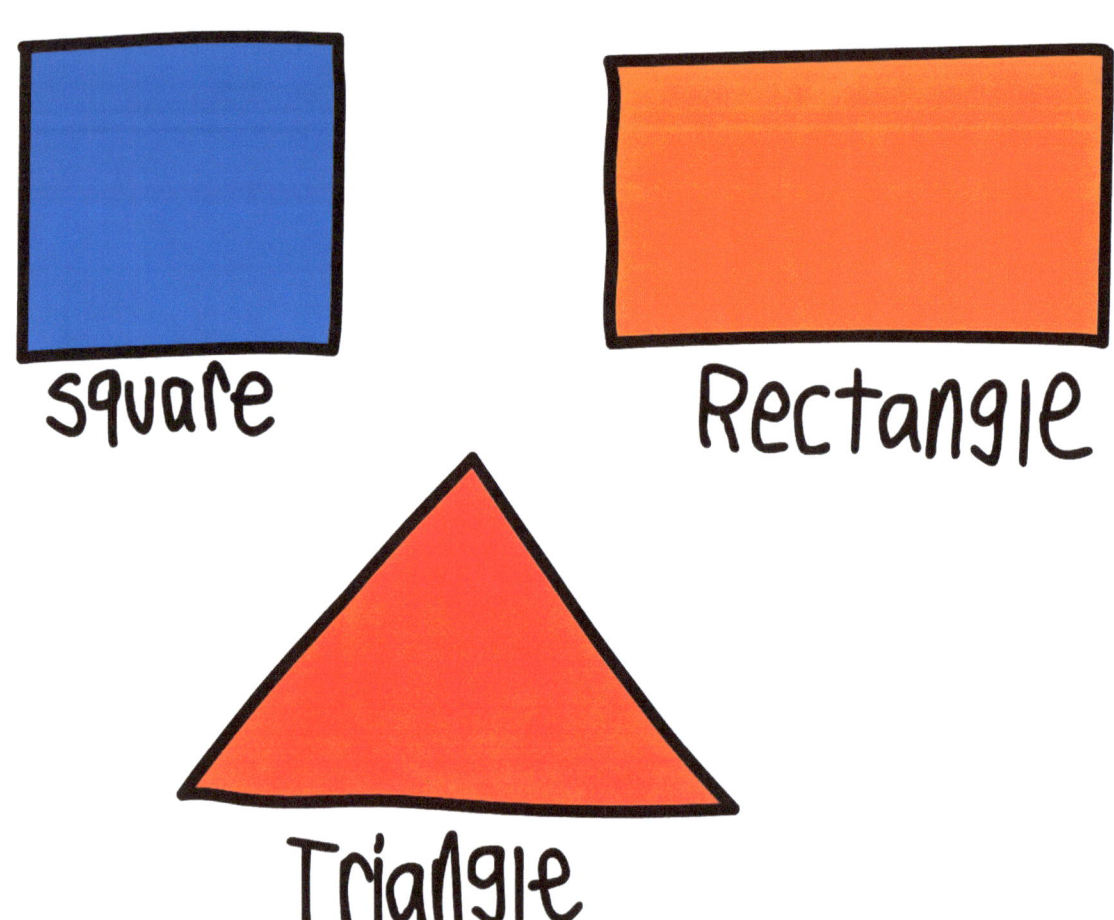

Planned

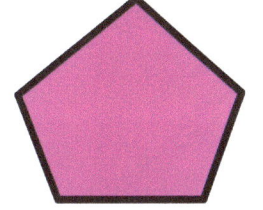 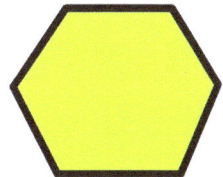 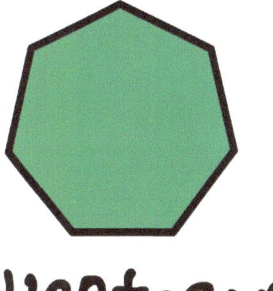

Pentagon   Hexagon   Heptagon

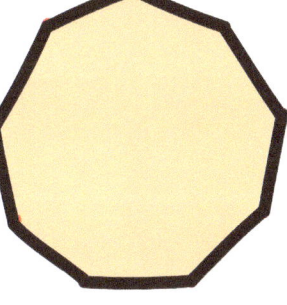 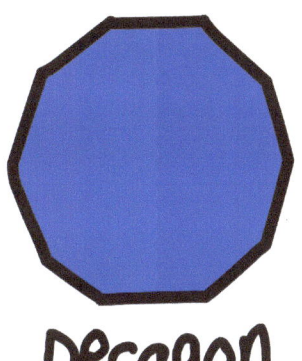

Octagon   Nonagon   Decagon

Keyed

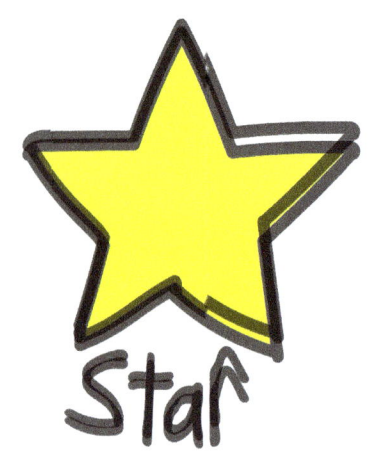
Star

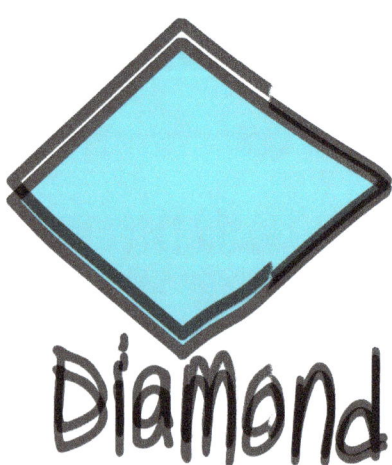
Diamond

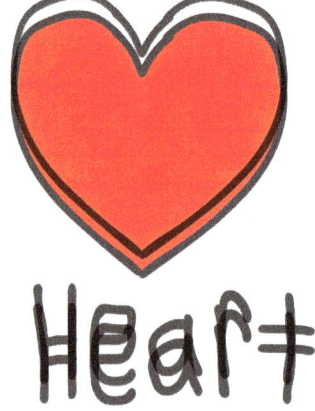
Heart

Chapter 4
Patterns & Lines

Basics

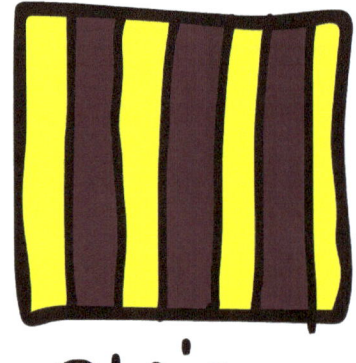
Stripes

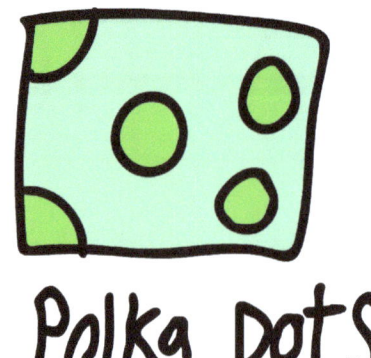
Polka Dots

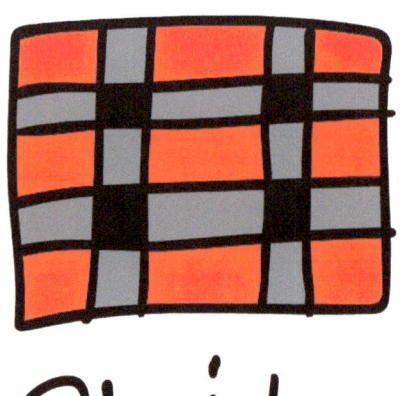
Plaid

Lines

zigzag   Straight   Spiral

Curve   Thin   Thick

Dotted lines   Squiggle

Chapter 5

More Wonderful Colors

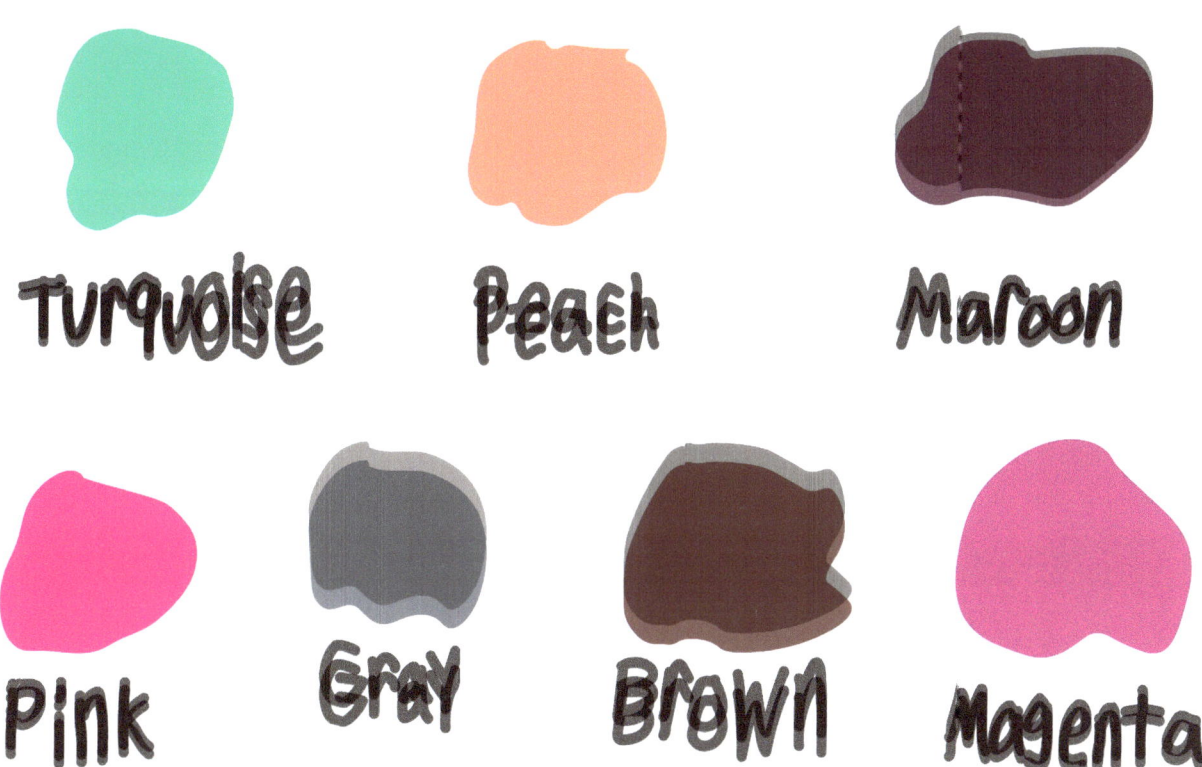

Chapter 6
Fundamentals of Art

Form

Perspective

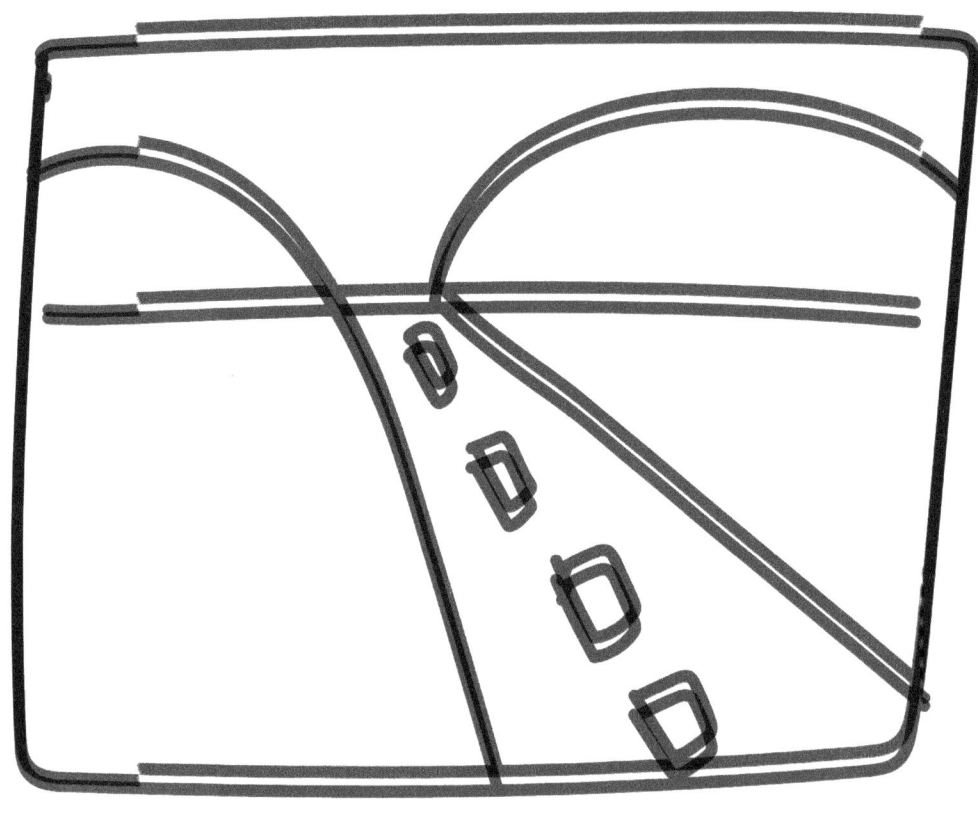

Anatomy

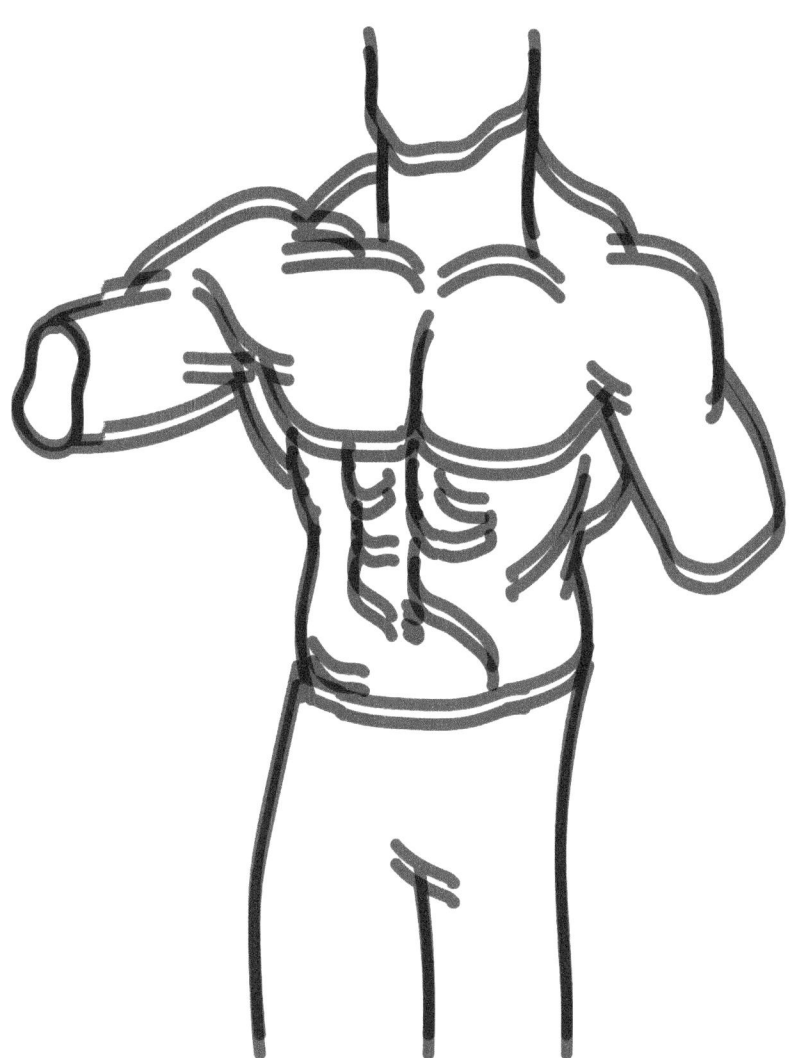

Composition

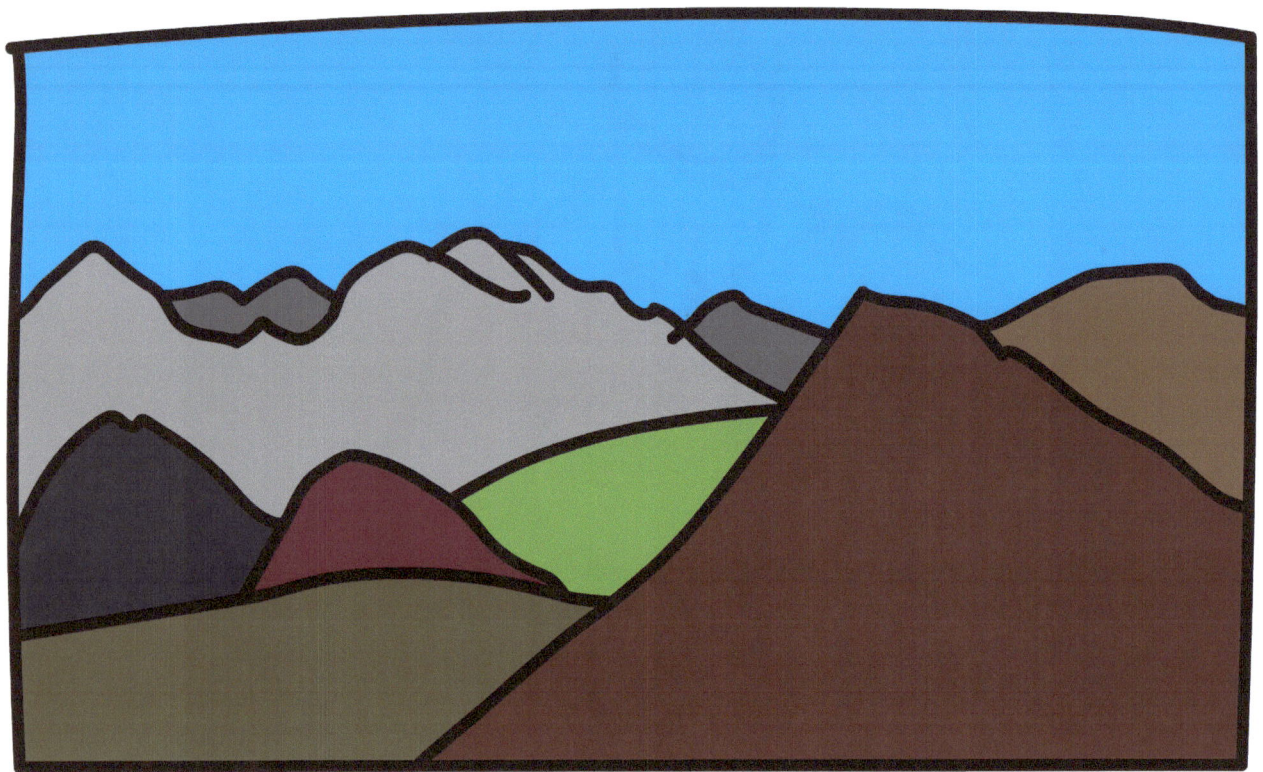

Conclusion

In Art, the Artists express themselves in many different ways for grand culture. It may have started in primitive culture from a long time ago, but you have to start somewhere.

In recent famous times these famous pieces of art can be shipped to art shows or art museums. Many artists travel from their native countries to show their expressions and feelings to give mood on what it would look like from their perspective.

We have come a long way since the dawn of man, the artistry of mankind has been brought to the public for 1,000's of years. The world of art has been a grand way to bring the future of many artists that live on from generation to legacy.

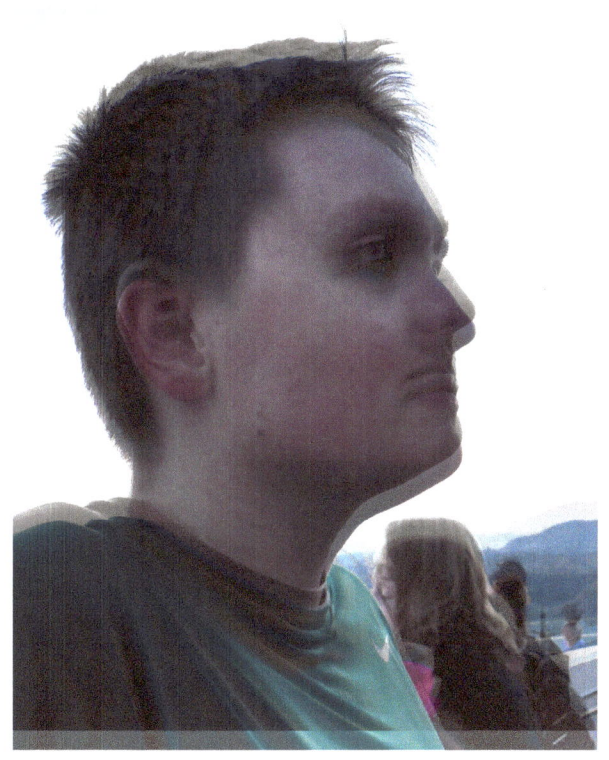

AUTHOR BIO

Harry Schad is a, 18 year old, native Missourian, filmmaker, animator, illustrator, and storyteller on the Autism Spectrum. He has produced a number of short films and greeting cards at Tink Tank Animate. This is Harry Schad's first publication. "Art is important to me because it is a part of my life since elementary school," Harry Schad.

www.ingramcontent.com/pod-product-compliance
Lightning Source LLC
Chambersburg PA
CBHW051940210526
45473CB00006B/2322